The Man in the Moon

Written by Daniel Shepard
Illustrated by Jesse Reich

Rigby · Saxon · Steck-Vaughn

www.HarcourtAchieve.com
1.800.531.5015

Contents

2

A Night at the Park

Elisa and her family enjoyed walking through the park to get away from the busy city. One cool summer evening they were sitting on a park bench and looking up at the night sky.

Elisa and her sister, Letty, loved to stare at the smiling Man in the Moon. Their father had told them many stories about that mysterious face.

As Elisa and Letty stared at the moon's face that night, they noticed that it was low in the sky and looked a little different.

"Elisa, do you notice something different about the Man in the Moon tonight?" whispered Letty.

"Yeah! His face looks kind of sad," Elisa replied. The Man in the Moon seemed to be frowning.

Elisa and Letty had often wondered what living on the moon would be like. For them, living on the moon would be a dream come true. They couldn't imagine why the Man in the Moon would be sad.

A Night on the Moon

The Man in the Moon looked out at the dark sky. It was a quiet night. But then, of course, it was always a quiet night on the moon. He looked out at Earth and wondered what it was like to live there. All his life he had lived on the moon. It was his home, but he was feeling lonely.

Each day and each night, life on the moon was the same. There was no wind, rain, or weather of any kind. There were no people or animals. There was dust and rocks, and that was all.

Star Light, Star Bright

"Living on Earth would be a dream come true! I'm tired of doing the same thing day after day," the Man in the Moon thought to himself. "And besides, I don't think anyone would notice if I were gone. If it weren't for the sun, no one would even see me."

So he looked out at his favorite shining star and made a wish. He whispered softly, "Star light, star bright, please grant this wish I wish tonight."

Then he closed his eyes and made his wish. "I wish I could visit Earth," he said.

Suddenly, his wish came true. The Man in the Moon shot out of the moon and tumbled toward Earth. "This is amazing!" he said to himself. "I'm finally going to Earth. This is going to be great!"

Down to Earth

When the Man in the Moon got to Earth, it was a beautiful day. There was so much to see and do. Everything was new to him. The first thing he did was take off his shoes and run through the grass in the park. Then he dipped his toes in a fountain.

"It's a great day!" a woman with a cart said.

"It sure is!" the Man in the Moon replied. "What do you have there?"

"It's the best ice cream in the city! Here, try it." The woman handed him a huge strawberry ice cream cone. The Man in the Moon had never tasted anything so creamy, sweet, and icy cold.

The Man in the Moon saw all of the things people could do with more gravity. He watched as people rode bikes, jogged, and skated. There was no way to keep a bike or skates on the ground on the moon.

"May I try your skates?" he asked two teenagers.

"Sure," one answered.

The Man in the Moon wobbled at first, but he soon got the hang of it. He was having so much fun! The Man in the Moon thanked the teenagers. Then he spent the rest of the day watching the world around him from a park bench.

As people passed by, he heard a child say, "I love the moon, Mommy. It's so beautiful!" Hearing this made the Man in the Moon happy. He looked up at his home and, for a second, he missed it.

Later, a family came along and sat down near the Man in the Moon. The family was looking out at the night sky when one little girl said sadly, "Daddy, something is wrong with the moon."

The other girl added, "Yesterday we saw the Man in the Moon frowning, and now he has disappeared!" The moon looked very plain.

"You're right. I don't see him," said their mother. The Man in the Moon looked up at the sky. He noticed how very empty the moon looked.

Home Sweet Home

The Man in the Moon never knew how much he had meant to people on Earth. He didn't think anyone would even notice that he had been gone. But now he knew that people cared.

"The moon is dusty, dry, and rocky," he thought. "But it's my home. Earth is beautiful, but it's not where I belong."

The Man in the Moon knew it was time for him to go. So he found his favorite star, and once again, he made a wish. But this time he wished to be back home on the moon.

In the blink of an eye, the Man in the Moon was back on the moon's surface. He was happy to be home. As he gazed at Earth, he felt a warm feeling in his heart.

"What an amazing time I had," he thought. "I will never forget it."

There had never been a brighter, happier face in the moon than there was that night. The Man in the Moon knew that people on Earth missed him when he was gone. Now he knew there were people on Earth who were probably looking up at him and smiling at that very moment. And this time, he was smiling back.

Close AND Turn

Index

Close AND Turn

Glossary

crater a giant bowl-shaped hole on the surface of the Moon

crescent a thin, curved shape that is one of the moon's phases

gravity a natural force that pulls things toward each other

moon any large, natural object that moves around a planet

orbit the movement of a planet or moon going around a sun or planet

phases the different shapes of the moon as we see them from Earth

surface the outside of something

temperature how hot or cold something is

tides the rise and fall of the level of the ocean

Many people talk about a "man in the moon."
They think the dark spots on the moon look
like a face. But these spots are simply shadows
of mountains and huge craters. Still, it's fun to
imagine!

What do you see when you look at the moon?

15

Moon Myths

People have told stories about the moon for thousands of years. In the past, people didn't know what the moon really was, so they made up stories.

Some thought the moon was a god or goddess. Many thought that there were animals or people living there. One Native American story even says that the moon is a hunter. This piece of art shows how they view the moon.

Moon Fact

The moon has less gravity than Earth. So, if you weighed 80 pounds on Earth, you would only weigh about 14 pounds on the moon!

Since 1969 more astronauts have been to the moon. They wore special suits, and had to bring air to breathe. Because there is so much less gravity on the moon than there is on Earth, they could bounce and flip as they looked around.

13

A Trip to the Moon

People had wanted to visit the moon for thousands of years. This dream finally came true in 1969 when the United States sent three astronauts to the moon. This was called the *Apollo 11* mission. It took 102 hours and 45 minutes for the spaceship to reach the moon.

When it finally arrived, Neil Armstrong became the first person to ever walk on the moon. As he stepped onto the surface he said, "That's one small step for man, one giant leap for mankind."

This footprint made by the astronaut Neil Armstrong will be on the moon for billions of years. There is no wind, rain, or snow on the moon to move the dust around and cover it.

The moon's **temperature** changes from very hot to very cold. It goes up to 230°F when it is heated by the sun. Without the sun, the temperature goes down to −292°F!

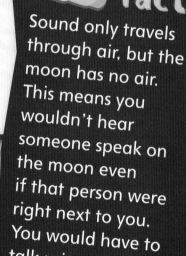

Moon Fact

Sound only travels through air, but the moon has no air. This means you wouldn't hear someone speak on the moon even if that person were right next to you. You would have to talk using a radio!

11

What's on the Moon?

The moon has no water or air. Because of this, you can't breathe on the moon and there are no plants, animals, people, or life of any kind. So what is on the moon?

The moon has a rocky, dusty **surface**. Billions of years ago, giant rocks hit the moon's surface. That is why the moon has huge **craters** on it. These craters have hardly changed over billions of years.

High Tide

Look at the picture above. It was taken during high tide. Now look at the picture below. It was taken at the same place during low tide. Can you see the difference?

Low Tide

9

The Moon and the Tides

Did you know that the moon affects the world's oceans? The moon's **gravity** pulls on the oceans. This creates **tides**. The ocean water comes far up onto the shore (high tide), or moves far away from the shore (low tide).

When it's low tide, you can see starfish, crabs, and shells that have been pushed up by the high tide. Then when high tide comes back, the water covers them up again. This happens twice each day as the moon's gravity pulls the ocean waters.

8

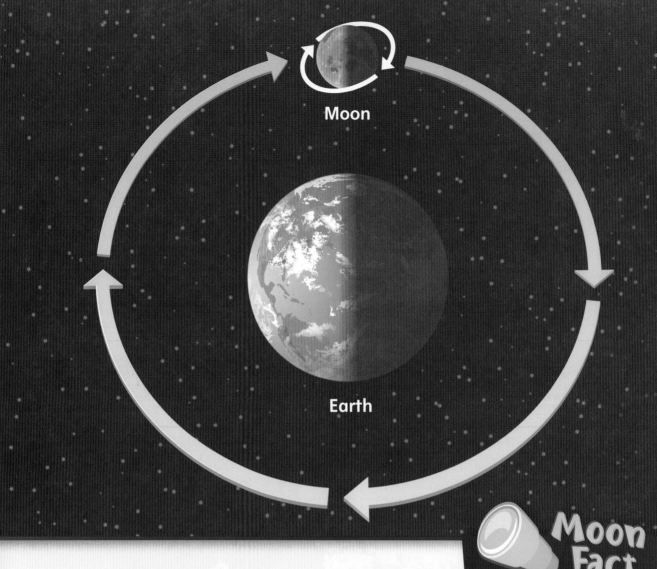

Moon

Earth

The moon moves around Earth in the same way that Earth moves around the sun. It takes one year for Earth to finish its orbit around the sun. But it only takes about one month for the moon to orbit around Earth.

The moon spins as it orbits around Earth. It makes one complete spin for each orbit around Earth. That's why we only see one side of the moon.

Moon Fact

No one ever saw the other side of the moon until 1959. That was when the first photographs of the other side of the moon were sent back to Earth.

7

Moon's Orbit

Sun

Every month, the moon goes through all of its phases. Each phase shows us more of the moon as it gets closer to becoming full. We see less of the moon as it returns to a new moon. Then it starts all over again.

Look at the diagram above. Can you tell what phase the moon is in?

Moon Phases

New   Crescent   Half   Full

Look at the pictures above. They show the different shapes, or **phases**, of the moon. A new moon is when we can't see the moon at all, because Earth is blocking the sun's light from shining on the moon. When the moon looks like a thin, curved line it is called a **crescent**. The next phase is a half moon. Finally, when the moon is a big circle in the sky it is called a full moon.

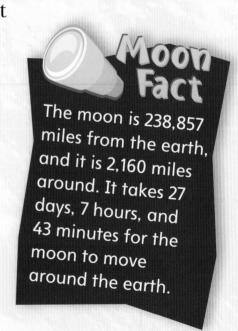

Moon Fact

The moon is 238,857 miles from the earth, and it is 2,160 miles around. It takes 27 days, 7 hours, and 43 minutes for the moon to move around the earth.

5

Moon Phases

The moon shines brightly, but did you know that it doesn't make its own light? The moon is lit by the sun. The moon seems to change its shape because the sun shines on different parts of it.

Night after night, it might look like the moon is changing, but that's not really happening. The shape of the moon looks like it changes because the moon **orbits**, or circles, around Earth.

4

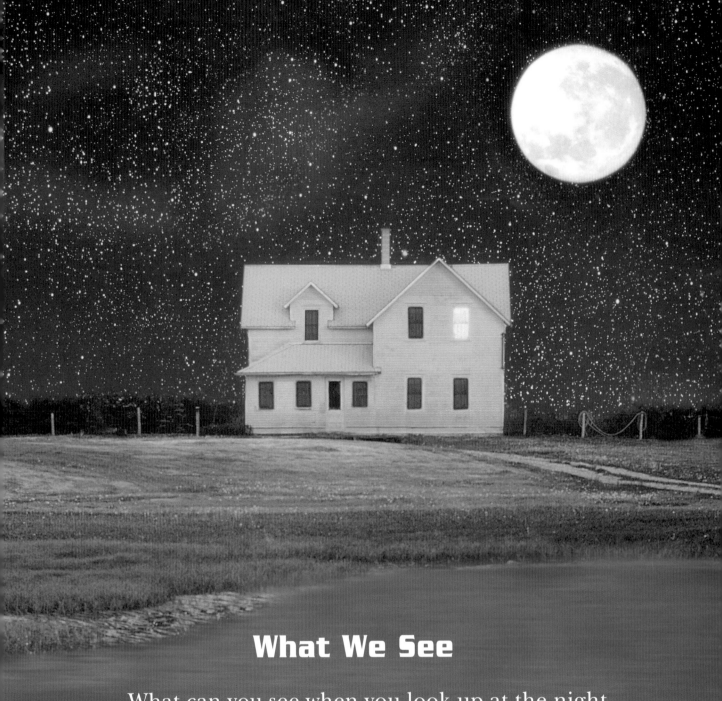

What We See

What can you see when you look up at the night sky? You see stars twinkling and some planets shining. And you can also see the **moon** shining brightly against a dark sky. The moon is closer to us than any star or planet.

But what is this giant shape in the sky we call the moon? Let's find out.

3

Contents

Our Moon

Written by Daniel Shepard

Harcourt Achieve
Rigby • Saxon • Steck-Vaughn

www.HarcourtAchieve.com
1.800.531.5015